THE W·O·V·E·N LABEL BOOK

RUVEN FEDER   J.M. GLASMAN

THE WOVEN LABEL BOOK

Editions

YOCAR FEDER

- Publié par Logos-Designs
EDITIONS YOCAR FEDER
153, Rue Saint-Martin
75003 Paris - France
- Copyright © 1989 Yocar Feder
- Toutes les étiquettes contenues dans ce livre sont
  reproduites avec l'autorisation de leurs auteurs ou leurs
  ayants droit ou de leurs ayants cause (fabricants,
  fournisseurs d'étiquettes, etc.), et l'auteur de cet ouvrage
  ne saurait être poursuivi pour toute reproduction illicite
  ou délictueuse éventuelle de dessins ou modèles protégés
  par les Lois.
- ISBN 2 906792 004
- Edité par Yocar Feder
  Conception graphique Valérie Envain
  Maquettiste Christophe Delamare
  Textes Olivier Lamour
  Illustrations Francisco Moreno
  Coordination Catherine Mougin
  Photocomposition Compact, Paris
  Imprimé et relié par Sirivatana, Bangkok
  Etiquette tissée de couverture réalisée par Mion Italie.

- Published by Logos-Designs
EDITIONS YOCAR FEDER
153, Rue Saint-Martin
75003 Paris - France
Copyright © Yocar Feder
- ISBN 2 906792 004
- Published by Yocar Feder
Graphic conception: Valérie Envain
Lay-out: Christophe Delamare
Text: Olivier Lamour
Illustrations: Francisco Moreno
English translations: Louise Guiney
Coordination: Catherine Mougin
Photocomposition : Compact, Paris
Printed and bound by Sirivatana, Bangkok
Woven label on cover by Mion Italia.

Ce livre est le début d'une série qui présente les meilleures réalisations d'étiquettes tissées récentes et anciennes. Les prochains livres que nous souhaitons éditer concerneront d'autres genres d'étiquettes imprimées, sur carton, P.V.C., caoutchouc, etc., et peut-être sur les badges! Fabricants, collectionneurs, contactez-nous pour nous proposer vos "petites merveilles".

This book is the first in a series presenting the best woven labels, past and present.
The next books we hope to be putting out will cover other types of printed labels - on cardboard, P.V.C., rubber, etc. And we also want to cover badges! We're calling on all manufacturers, and all collectors to get in touch with us and tell us about their "little gems".

Logos Designs
EDITIONS YOCAR FEDER
153, Rue Saint-Martin
75003 PARIS - FRANCE
Tél. 42 78 38 20

Sommaire

CONTENTS

- Publié par Logos-Designs
EDITIONS YOCAR FEDER
153, Rue Saint-Martin
75003 Paris - France
- Copyright © 1989 Yocar Feder

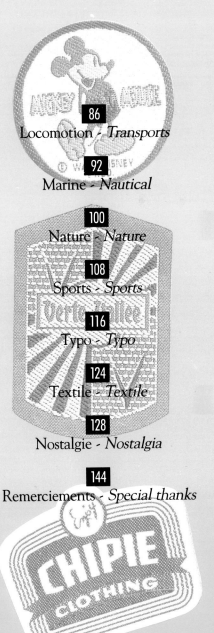

Véritable phénomène de société, l'étiquette est la plus directe, la plus simple et la meilleure des publicité. La plupart des stylistes de mode s'en sont aperçus et s'en servent comme d'un véhicule de communication à part entière. Et pourtant, l'étiquette revient de loin. Souvenez-vous. Il n'y a pas si longtemps encore, lorsqu'on acceptait une griffe sur sa chemise, même minuscule, on se faisait traiter d'"homme sandwich". Les temps ont changé. Bien vite! Chipie a bombardé d'étiquettes l'extérieur de tous ses vêtements, Marithé et François Girbaud ont même, les premiers, cousu une étiquette sur la braguette de leurs pantalons sans que personne ne s'en émeuve et aujourd'hui, les jeunes japonais réclament par bataillons entiers de badges et des blasons Chevignon. Explication de ce brusque changement de mentalité? L'étiquette "accessoirise" le vêtement. Elle lui rend une identité mise à mal par l'uniformisation croissante de l'habillement.

Mais foin des savants discours socio-ethnologiques. Ne comptez pas sur nous pour les doctes analyses. Pourquoi? Parce que l'incroyable ascension des marques et de leurs étiquettes dans le prêt à porter, c'est un peu notre métier. De plus nous éditons ensemble "le" cahier de tendances de l'étiquette. Le WOVEN LABEL BOOK doit servir à autre chose. Au plaisir des yeux! Celui de montrer de belles images, que nous avons chinées aux quatre coins du monde. Dans les ateliers ultra-modernes de l'un des plus grands fabricants du Japon, comme dans les greniers centenaires et poussiéreux d'une maison française.

Mais aussi en Espagne, en Italie, en Belgique, en Allemagne… et ailleurs. Il y avait urgence! On a tout vu ces derniers temps : des "griffes" mal tissées, dessinées n'importe comment, agrémentées de couleurs ringardes et produites à la va-vite! des laideurs qui ne doivent pas nous faire oublier les chefs-d'œuvre de finesse réunis dans cet ouvrage. Par thèmes. D'abord car c'est un classement dans l'air du temps, ensuite parce que sur les étiquettes, ce sont les mythologies dominantes de cette fin de siècle, que l'on retrouve : rêves de voyage, d'exotisme, d'authenticité… On peut encore dire qu'il existait déjà des livres sur les boîtes d'allumettes, sur le bowling, les cravates ou les chemises hawaïennes et rien ou peu de choses sur les étiquettes tissées… ça nous agaçait! Enfin ce style de bouquin est toujours fabriqué à New York, Londres ou Tokyo. Pourquoi pas à Paris pour une fois? Cocorico.

RUVEN FEDER & JEAN-MICHEL GLASMAN

Labels have become a social phenomenon, the most direct, the simplest, and the best medium for the advertising message. Most fashion stylists are well aware of this, and now use labels as "total communication". But it wasn't always this way.

We all remember the time not so long ago when even a tiny label on the outside of a shirt made people feel like "sandwich boards". Time marches on - at a gallop! Chipie has plastered labels all over the outside of their garments, and Marithé and François Girbaud pioneered the label sewn outside the fly on their trousers... and nobody batted an eye! In Japan, trendy teenagers are voting en masse for Chevignon badges and shields. Why this sudden change in attitudes? The answer is that an eye-catching label accessorizes a garment, giving it the kind of unique identity that the increasingly homogeneous clothing styles of today lack.

We aren't scholars or sociologists, however, and we can't provide an objective analysis of the label phenomenon. Why not? Because labels are our business, and the meteoric rise of trademarks and labels in the apparel industry is a sourse of pride and satisfaction to us. Joint publishers of "the" logo and label design trend book, we are here giving the whole subject a closer look. THE WOVEN LABEL BOOK is designed primarily as a feast for the eyes. A wonderful collection of designs we have scoured the world for, from the ultra-modern workshops of one of the foremost label manufacturers in Japan, to the dusty, antique attics of a French company with its roots firmly fixed in the traditions of the past. We went to Spain, we went to Italy, we went to Belgium and Germany... and we didn't go a minute too soon! The field has become so crowded, quality is suffering. It's time to weed out the good from the bad, the excellent from the so-so. Forget every label you've ever seen that was poorly designed, poorly made, or in bad taste. Turn the pages of this book, and feast your eyes on masterpieces of label design, arranged by category. The themes we've chosen reflect the times we live in, and the labels here reflect the dominant mytholo-

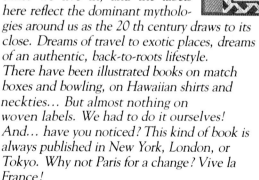

gies around us as the 20 th century draws to its close. Dreams of travel to exotic places, dreams of an authentic, back-to-roots lifestyle.

There have been illustrated books on match boxes and bowling, on Hawaiian shirts and neckties... But almost nothing on woven labels. We had to do it ourselves! And... have you noticed? This kind of book is always published in New York, London, or Tokyo. Why not Paris for a change? Vive la France!

RUVEN FEDER AND JEAN-MICHEL GLASMAN

Historique

BACKGROUND

Commencerons-nous en 1805, avec l'invention de Joseph-Marie Jacquard? Non! Sa fameuse "mécanique a tisser" est un peu trop lointaine. Alors devrons-nous entamer ce court historique par les premières étiquettes de notre collection? Des images pieuses tissées sur soie qu'on pourrait prendre pour des gravures, des écussons pour les scouts ou encore des bandes décorées destinées aux bérets des marins au début du siècle… Pas davantage. Pourquoi? Parce que la véritable histoire des étiquettes commence dans les années 50.

Un des premiers métiers à tisser du temps de Jacquard. *One of the first Jacquard-era looms.*

Depuis la fin de la seconde guerre mondiale jusqu'au début des trente glorieuses, elle n'a servi qu'à des "chemisiers habilleurs" qui se sont fait de la publicité gratuitement sur le dos de leurs clients en tissant le nom de leur boutique, "Paris Nouveauté", "route de Rennes à Laval", ou plus moderne encore, "La chemise Kiplait".

La réclame balbutie. L'étiquette aussi. Elles se développeront ensemble. Car si la griffe des petits chemisiers de province a peu d'avenir, il n'en va pas de même pour les marques. Nous vous avons retrouvé les ancêtres du célébrissime crocodile de Lacoste. Mordant! Mais les sigles discrets et les vignettes techniques vont bientôt être supplantés. Par les étiquettes décoratives. En France, c'est Chipie qui lance le mouvement. Presque par hasard. Un stonewashing un peu trop vigoureux endommage tout un stock de jeans et de salopettes. Il faut boucher les trous. Avec quoi? Gagné? C'est le succès. Aujourd'hui, Chipie coud plus de quatre millions d'étiquettes chaque année et vend dans ses boutiques, des pochettes pleines… d'étiquettes!

Entre-temps, les petits bouts de Jacquard ont tout investi : les cols, le dos, les manches, les jambes, la ceinture et même… la braguette. Ils ont aussi acquis le statut d'œuvre d'art avec la reproduction tissée d'un tableau d'Hokusaï au dos des jeans Kenzo ou, avec la création par M. et F. Girbaud d'une somptueuse étiquette qui raconte l'histoire du lin et sert de doublure à un blouson. Du coup, quelques fabricants commencent à protéger leurs étiquettes comme leurs brevets les plus secrets. Certains autres, ici même, leur consacrent un livre et d'autres encore… le lisent. Et ça n'est qu'un début!

Should we go all the way back to 1805 and Joseph-Marie Jacquard's trail-blazing

invention? No! Jacquard's famous "weaving machine" is just a little too far-distant. Well, then, should we start our history lessons with the first labels in our collection? Those meticulously woven silk images that could almost be engravings – badges for the Boy Scouts or the embroidered strips that went on sailors' hats at the turn of the century… No, we won't start with them, either. Why not? Because the real history of the label doesn't begin until the 1950s. From the end of World War II up until the beginning of the label's glorious thirty years' rise to fame, the tiny piece of embroidery was used primarily by fancy shirtmakers who put a little bit of free advertising on their customers' backs, usually just the name of the boutique – "Paris Nouveauté", from "the Route de Rennes to Laval", or the more modern "La Chemise Kiplait".

Advertising was still in its infancy, and so were labels. The two grew up together. The trademarks of obscure provincial shirtmakers may not have had much of a future, but the major brand image was straining at the starting line, all ready to take off. We've discovered the grand-daddy of the world-renowned Lacoste alligator – there's a tail to be told! – but discreet trademarks and labels just giving information on size, etc., were soon to be put in the shade by a new arrival on the scene: the decorative label.

"Chipie" spearheaded the movement in France. Almost by accident. A lot of jeans and overalls was subjected to a stone-washing and someone overdid it a little. Something had to be done to cover up the holes. What? Inspiration! A new star is born! Today Chipie sews up a storm of four million labels annually and in its boutiques sells bags full of… labels!

Since then, these tiny bits of Jacquard have invaded everything: collars, backs, sleeves, legs, belts and even… the trouser fly. They've also acquired status: there's a woven reproduction of a painting by Hokusaï on the back of Kenzo jeans, and M.' and F. Girbaud have designed a magnificent label with the history of linen on it which is used as the lining for a blouson jacket. Labels have gotten so hot, some manufacturers have begun protecting them as they would a valuable patent. And some people – us, for example – are writing whole books about them, which lots of other people actually read! And this is just the beginning…

Création d'une

DESIGNING A LABEL

THIS GAR

Aut
H

P as de surprise : tout commence par le dessin. Aux graphistes des studios de création, tout est permis. Ils peuvent puiser leur inspiration partout : dans les livres, les revues illustrées, la mode de la rue, le cinéma, les phénomènes de société comme la montée de l'écologie... Toutes les tendances sont bonnes à suivre. Actuellement, l'ère des pilotes de chasse et du Fun cèdent la place aux dessins primitifs, à l'orientalisme, à la nature. Seule contrainte : se conformer aux produits et à l'image de marque du client.

Ensuite vient le choix des couleurs sélectionnées sur la gamme de teintes de fils de chacun des fabricants d'étiquettes. Ici s'achève la création propre à l'étiquette... et commence l'attente fébrile de la carte "JACQUARD". Mais ça c'est la techno.

étiquette

Y es, it all begins with the design. The graphic artists working in design studios can do anything they want. They get their inspiration from all kinds of things: books, glossy magazines, street fashion, film, and sociological phenomena like the current interest in ecology. Everything is grist for their mill. Currently, the fighter pilot and fun looks are being supplanted by primitive designs, orientalism, and nature. There is only one constant in label design: you have to be consistent with the product, and with the client's brand image.

Once the design has been approved, then comes time to select the colors from the ranges available at the label manufacturer's. This is the finishing touch... followed by a period of breath-holding while waiting for the "carte jacquard" to arrive. But that's another story, one that comes under "techno"...

Techno

TECHNO

Pour le graphiste et le fabricant de prêt-à-porter, la partie technique est la plus stressante. Avant de

livrer à leur admiration la première série d'environ un millier de pièces qui révèlera leur petit chef-d'œuvre tissé, la fameuse "carte Jacquard" met une bonne semaine à se faire perforer. Mieux vaut qu'elle soit précise, car lorsque le métier s'ébranle, alimenté par ses quelques 150.000 fils, rien ne peut plus l'arrêter.

Les impatients peuvent désormais s'épargner cet insupportable suspense grâce aux ordinateurs graphiques qui, en trois ou quatre heures, offrent une simulation parfaite, couleur et armature comprise. De plus, l'informatisation des "cartes Jacquard" devrait en rendre l'usage plus aisé. Enfin, dans les plus récentes innovations, la plus intéressante semble bien être la découpe aux ultra-sons qui permet de donner toutes les formes voulues aux étiquettes, sans problème d'ourlet.
Et nous ne sommes qu'à l'aube du troisième millénaire…

For the graphic designer and the ready-to-wear manufacturer, the technical stage of label design is the most stressful. Before they can stand in admiration before the first completed series of some thousand pieces representing their little gem of a woven masterpiece, they have to wait for the notorious "jacquard card", which takes a good week to punch out. And a whole week is none

La maquette est scannée sur ordinateur. Les dernières modifications se font sur celui-ci avant l'accord du client.
The model is scanned by computer. Final changes are carried out on the computer prior to customer approval.

too long, since if the card isn't exactly right, the loom with its 150000 threads will get into a terrible tangle – and nothing will be able to stop it.

For people who just can't wait that long, there is another solution: they can look at a computer simulation of the design-color and weave included – that takes only three or four hours to produce. Computer Assisted Jacquard Cards are also easier to use. With the latest technology, not only is the period of suspense diminished dramatically, but the graphic software will also provide super-sonic cross-sections. The problem of the hem is eliminated, and the label can be viewed from any angle or in any size.

It's fantastic... but it's just a start. After all, we're barely at the dawn of the third millenium...

BARRIO GOTICO
BARCELONA

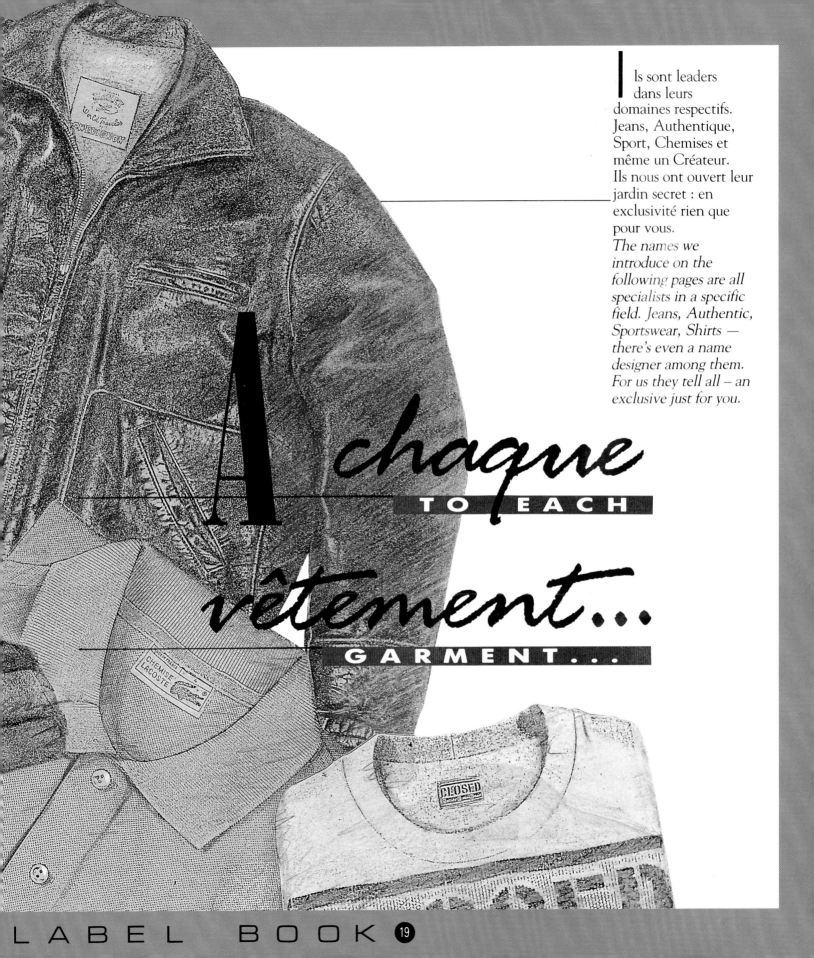

Ils sont leaders dans leurs domaines respectifs. Jeans, Authentique, Sport, Chemises et même un Créateur. Ils nous ont ouvert leur jardin secret : en exclusivité rien que pour vous.

The names we introduce on the following pages are all specialists in a specific field. Jeans, Authentic, Sportswear, Shirts — there's even a name designer among them. For us they tell all – an exclusive just for you.

A chaque
TO EACH

vêtement...
GARMENT...

Authentique

AUTHENTIC

"Jean story"

Du blouson aviateur en cuir vieilli de l'armée américaine, Chevignon a développé son histoire en créant plusieurs lignes de prêt-à-porter : CONQUEST : sportswear jeans, chemises et maille; TOGS UNLIMITED : doudounes, parkas et vêtements sportifs; STUDZ : les classiques de la ville GIRL et CHEVIGNON KIDS pour l'enfant. Chaque département est identifié par sa griffe à travers les différents thèmes de sa collection.

"Be free, go classic !"

Starting with the antiqued leather American Airforce flight jacket, Chevignon has gone on to shape its history around a number of ready-to-wear lines: CONQUEST: Sportswear jeans, shirts, and knits; TOGS UNLIMITED: Quilted outerwear, parkas, and sportswear; STUDZ: Townwear classics; GIRL and CHEVIGNON KIDS for children. Each line has its own trademark for the different themes in the collections.

"Children line"

Chevignon

OLD AMERICA'S FAVORITE LABEL

"Sporting time"

"Ladies too..."

Chemises

SHIRTS

La chemise, un grand classique. Central Park a su imposer son style, et créer une gamme authentique d'étiquettes en suivant l'évolution des tendances et des saisons.
Chaque vignette se veut intemporelle afin de pouvoir harmoniser une multitude de produits. Et chacun de ces modèles s'enrichit en vieillissant.

Shirts are classics. But "Central Park" has put its mark on shirts with a fresh, authentic line of labels reflecting current fashion trends and the season. Each of the labels is general enough to go with a host of different products, and they all improve with age.

W O V E N

L e créateur de l'étiquette "closed" sur la braguette (positionnement déposé) a offert pour l'été 87, cette somptueuse histoire du lin. Etiquette gigantesque qui servait de doublure à certains blousons de leur marque "Momentodue". Une vignette invitait carrément à "lire son blouson". Une autre aurait pu inciter à retourner sa veste.

MARITHÉ & FRANÇOIS GIRBAUD

T he designer of the "closed" trouser fly label (position patented) now brings us this sumptuous history of linen for Summer 1987. This gigantic label will be used to line some of the "Momentodue" make blouson jackets. These are jackets with a real story to tell... it's enough to make you into a "turncoat"!

Jeans
JEANS

Avec Chipie, c'est à un précurseur que l'on a affaire.

Au début des années 70, la marque est la première à donner à l'étiquette une importance autre que celle d'une simple identification.

Pour Chipie, en effet, l'étiquette est bien plus que cela; elle est travaillée et pensée en accord avec vêtement.

Elle devient ainsi le support d'une idée ou d'un thème. Chaque vêtement a sa propre griffe, qui comme lui, ne vit qu'une saison; hormis les basics qui eux conservent leur griffe d'origine. D'où l'impact formidable des modèles patchés Chipie, sur l'endroit, l'étiquette ne se cache plus, elle se montre et devient un signe de reconnaissance.

C hipie is a pace-setter in the field.

In the early 70s, Chipie was the first to feature labels as more than just a means of identification. Chipie believes a label is much more - and that it should be designed and developed in terms of the style of the garment.

A label should project and idea or a theme. Every garment hat its own individual image, one with a life span of just one season. Basics last longer, so does their image. And this is what made the

Chipie models with labels sewn on the outside so fantastically successful - the label came out of hiding and - pioneered by Chipie - is now an image-maker recognized by the consumer.

Jeans
JEANS

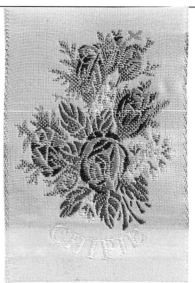

HAND WASHABLE
ALOHA SHIR7S
HAND SCREENED
Single Needle throughout

DEPUIS 1967

QUALITE
CHIPIE
BRODERIE

CHIPIE®
AUTHENTIC
DENIM
WESTERN WEAR
CHIPIE JEANS
of FRENCH STYLE

CHIPIE

Chipie Rodéo

FRENCH'S PRIDE   100% PREP
CHIPIE
Wintermaster

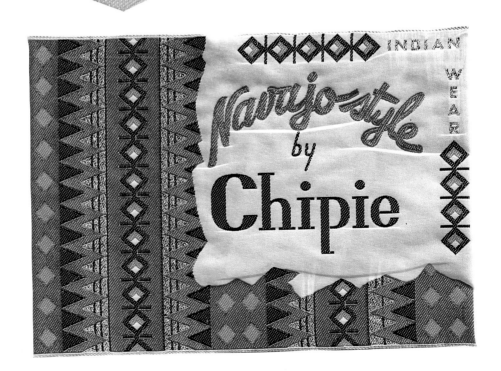

INDIAN WEAR
Navajo-style
by
Chipie

Jeans
JEANS

Une ligne de produits dérivés de la fripe U.S. avec une coupe particulièrement définie, des produits simples et authentiques. L'image de Liberto est liée à ses jeans et ses pantalons qui sont des purs produits basics.

Outre le "basic", une collection nouvelle et complète qui est développée chaque saison sur un thème bien défini. Les étiquettes suivent…

A line based on U.S.-style period apparel, with a distinctive cut - simple and authentic. The Liberto image is focused on its basic jeans and pants lines.
In addition to the "Basic" line, a new comprehensive collection is developed each season on a specific theme. The labels follow suit…

LIBERTO
ROYAL
BLUE

FABRIC SHRINKAGE NOT OVER

LIBERTO

means so much more

UNIVERSAL WESTERN STAR

Sport

SPORT

Un nom et un emblème qui parlent d'eux-mêmes...
Lacoste avec son crocodile, véritable légende, poursuit son irrésistible ascension depuis plus de 50 ans dans une discrétion de bon ton.
L'évolution des étiquettes sur sa "fameuse chemise" est plus sage, puisque dès l'origine, Lacoste a pris le parti de mettre en valeur avant tout son célèbre croco dile, devenu aujourd'-hui un mythe.

A name and emblème that speak volumes...
With the legendary alligator, Lacoste has for almost fifty years gained increasing fame for understated good taste.
Labels on the famed "Lacoste shirt" have changed little, since from the beginning Lacoste decided to feature the famous alligator that has today become a myth.

René Lacoste - 1927 au smash - Cette nouvelle étiquette sera destinée à une ligne jogging.
René Lacoste - a 1927 smash - This new label will go on a line of jogging apparel.

Thèmes
THEMES

Comment organiser une collection aussi riche que la nôtre? Le classement par thèmes est visuellement le plus esthétique. Il donne une juste idée de l'homogénéité des sources d'inspiration. Et puis, il est à la mode! Pour les collectionneurs les plus avertis, l'origine de chaque étiquette, ou presque, est indiquée en légende par un symbole propre à chaque fabricant. Bon voyage!

Ever wonder how to organize a collection as vast as this one? We decided to do it by theme, by far the most appealing method, visually. It gives an accurate idea of the key sources of inspiration. Also - everybody's doing it: For the real collector, the origin of all (or almost all) the labels is given in captions, using symbols. Have a good trip through the wonderful world of the woven label!

Années

FIFTIES

50

Un thème vieux comme le rock ! Se lassera-t-on un jour des pin-up, des belles américaines, des formes "cinquante". Les juniors ne nous démentiront pas...

A theme as old as... rock! Will we ever have enough of pin-up girls, big cars, and "fifties" design? Not if teenagers have anything to say about it...

STONE WASHED
SPECIAL AND FINISH
IN AT 9:00
OUT AT 5:00
PICKUP
and
DELIVERY
CALL
4-2111
Half
A FRESH NEW EXPERIENCE
HALF CORPORATION

Make it all-right!!
THE WORLD'S
MOST FAMOUS
TRADITIONAL AND
COMFORTABLE
GARMENT
High Class
Sportswear
CRACKER'S
TRADE MARK

Dance
PARTY BOYS!
H G S

Traditional
an ORIGINAL
FABRIQUE A GIE MAURICE

FAVORITE
on the
COLLEGE CAMPUS
SOLID
SHIRTS

Sabrina
THEY SELL
LIKE HOTCAKES
Nihon Half Corp.
Diploma Program
"20"
INCHES
LONG
HALF

Années
FIFTIES
50

THE ORIGINAL
Knitwear
by
STICKER®

CLOTHING LINE FOR MEN

Lemon

AUTHENTIC
NATURAL FABRIC

Italian Premium Quality Dress

MADE IN ITALY

SPECIAL WASH SERVICE
HOWARD W. MOORE

Half

GUARANTEED QUALITY MATERIAL
PROPORTIONED FIT FOR EXTRA COMFORT
Stone Washed And Special Finish
Dial 62-6236
IF No Answer Call 2-6389
HALF CORPORATION

REGULATION STYLE
UNIFORM OFFICER
Field Trousers
"*Chipie*" QUALITY

TRADE NATURAL SHAPE MARK
OUTSIDERS
FOR EVERY DAY

Samsonite
Luggage
SHWAYDER BROS., INC. DENVER

Années
FIFTIES
50

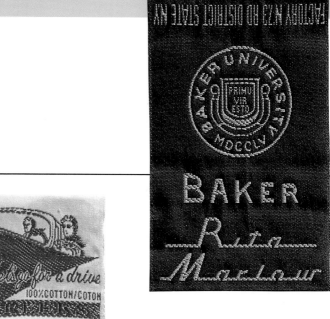

BAKER

Rita
Marlow

Let's go for a drive
100% COTTON/COTON

CHEVIGNON ®
MEN'S INFLUENCE
QUALITY AND TASTE
57½
MADE IN FRANCE
PARIS

DENIM WEARS
exclusive
DONOVAN
WORK CLOTHES

Into feet
INTERFACE
BY
ICEFIRE
GOOD and NICE
WE MAKE IT SURE AND PLEASE ENJOY IT

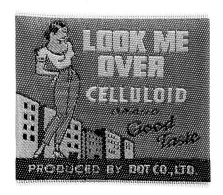

Aviateur
AVIATOR

L es "flying heroes" sont de vrais durs aux nerfs d'acier. Il existe toutes sortes d'objets du culte : cuirs, écussons, lunettes, casques… L'étiquette avait peu de chance d'échapper à cette envolée.

T he real man of steel is the "flying hero". Around him have accumulated all kinds of cult objects – leather accessories, badges, glasses, caps. The label was a sure thing to go with them.

The flying group
By
Fassianos

Man's clothing

Trade mark

Original design

GIORDANO

J and CO ®

TRADE   MARK

AUTHENTIQUE POINT SELLIER
(coutures à l'ancienne)

Roberto do Rego

CIMARRON
AMERICAN PILOT WEAR
STRICTLY FOR AVIATORS
Clothes airmen are proud to wear

Aviateur

AVIATOR

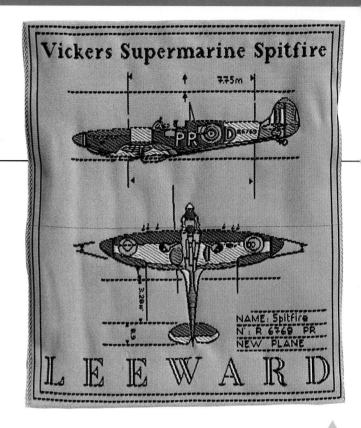

Vickers Supermarine Spitfire

7.75m

PR · D R6769

NAME: Spitfire
N°: R 6769 PR
NEW PLANE

LEEWARD

* ENTIRELY NEW MODEL
* SPEED SAFETY LUXURY
* ECONOMY RUGGEDLY
* CONSTRUCTED FOR
* LONG WEAR

Famous Basic

FLY

Parashooting

★ AVIATOR ★

PIERRE CRISTELL
Old Flight

GOOD LOOK

PANTS

EASY FIT

QUALITY   CLOTHES
DESIGNED FOR CONSTANT USE   Finest
AND DAILY PLEASURE   Value

QUALITY & COMFORT

AERO de CALYPSO
FLY ON THE WINGS OF PARADISE

Bande dessinée

CARTOONS

Ils sont tous là. Les vieux amis comme les nouveaux copains. Bécassine, Betty Boop et toute la bande à Disney ou les merveilleuses illustrations de Norman Rockwell… Et puis il y a cette originalité japonaise, mélange tissé et carton… Et aussi ces étiquettes, qui racontent une histoire. Il ne leur manque que la parole…

They're all here. The old familiar faces and the new kids on the block. Bécassine, Betty Boop, and all the wonderful Disney and Norman Rockwell creations… plus the fantastically original Japanese slant… weaving combined with cardboard… and labels that tell a story… if only they could really speak…

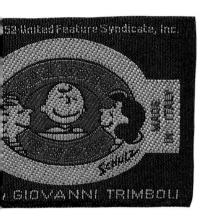

Bande dessinée
CARTOONS

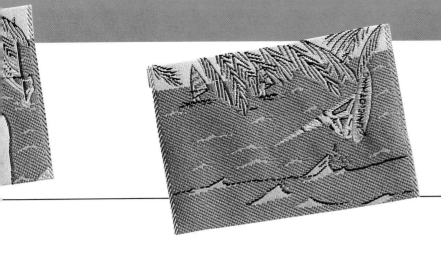

Bande dessinée
CARTOONS

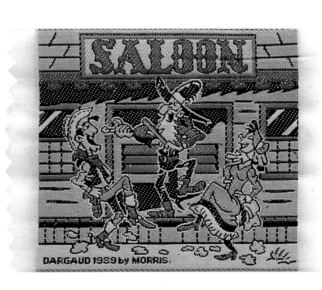

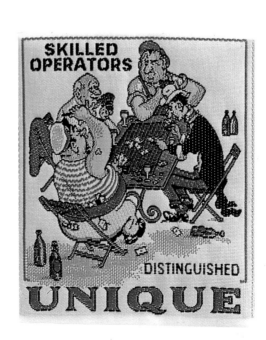

Ethnique
ETHNIC

E lles évoquent des ambiances lointaines plutôt que des voyages. Les Papous, les Mayas, les rites indonésiens… Elles décrivent des folklores colorés et s'appliquent de préférence sur des vêtements d'été.

T hese are the labels evoking the exotic climes at the end of the trip. Papuans, Mayas, Indonesian folk ritual… colorful and entrancing, they are designed to go on summer clothing.

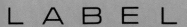

Ethnique
ETHNIC

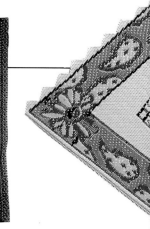

Far-West

FAR-WEST

L'authenticité, quand on pense aux jean's, c'est le Far West, les pionniers, la ruée vers l'or, la guerre de sécession. La toile Denim n'a pas démérité : elle résiste aussi bien à l'usage qu'à la mode !

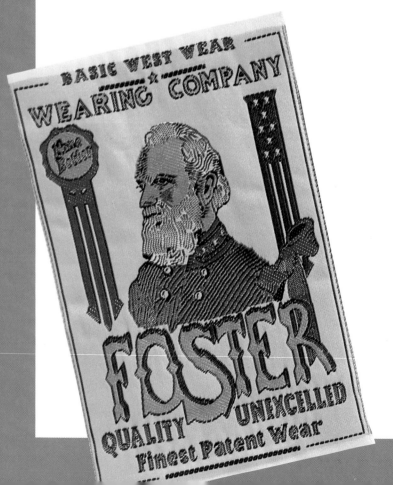

Authentic", when we're talking about jeans, means the Far West, the pioneers, the gold rush, the American Civil War. Denim was right there for all of them – timeless, hard-wearing, always in style.

PACIFIC TRAIL

Riders

ONLY SELECTED MATERIALS HAVE BEEN USED

WE ALWAYS ASK FOR THE BEST

DENIM

MADE TO PERFECT STANDARDS

JACKET

Exquisite Garment

THE KLONDIKE GOLD RUSH

This wear is exciting good.

Daring design from original creators.

We present the casual wear. Try it for something more.

THE KLONDYKE'S Extra GOLD MINES

DAWSON JE

Alaska Gold Fields ????

Miramar

UFO style

GOLD MINERS EQUIPMENT MADE IN SPAIN

NEW WASH

Far-West

FAR-WEST

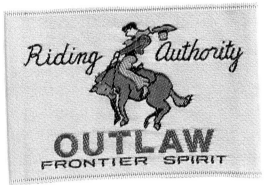

Faune
FAUNA

Notre zoo est complet.
Une véritable arche de
Noé! Nous avons dû classifier
ces animaux par genre. Mais
c'est un livre entier qu'il nous
aurait fallu…

Our zoo is full. Our Noah's
Ark is ready to set sail…
we have all the animals, all
the species… but we really
need a whole book just for
them!

This is a true love

LEATHER COMPANY

Expressly for G.b.Sportelli

Trade Mark

THE BEST OF
WEBB
KHAKI
WEBB
KHAKI

Rhinoceros

Faune
FAUNA

Faune

FAUNA

Faune
FAUNA

Globe

GLOBE

U n autre classique! Le
style expédition, safari,
aventurier, Indiana Jones,
Banana Republic est un
indémodable. Le globe
terrestre en est une constante.
Mais on aurait pu intituler ce
chapitre "Art of Travel".

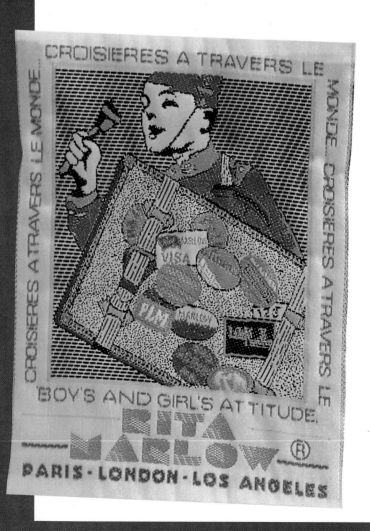

A nother classic! An
Indiana Jones' expedition
to some exotic Banana
Republic... always in the
headlines! The world will
always beckon... and we
could have called this chapter
the "Art of Travel".

Globe
GLOBE

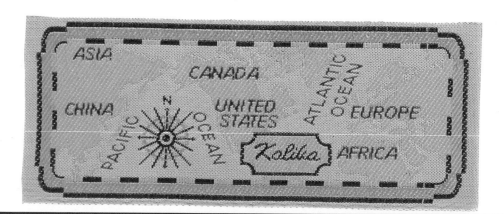

Globe
GLOBE

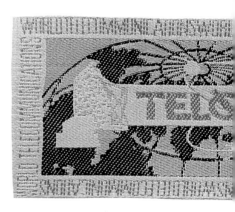

ONLY BASIG
Since *Big Star All over the world* 1975
MADEBY JEANS

RR 1881
CERRUTI SPORT
for a sportswear quietly to which
and conceived to live in perfect
harmony with the nature and
above all with the hardest
conditions of winter
sport.

TRADITION COMFORT
BAXTER
ORIGINAL SHIRTING

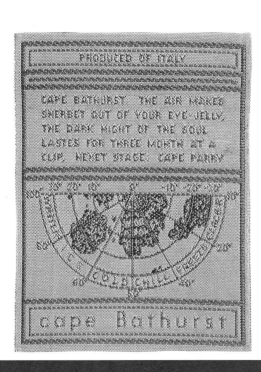

PRODUCED OF ITALY

CAPE BATHURST, THE AIR MAKES
SHERBET OUT OF YOUR EYE-JELLY,
THE DARK NIGHT OF THE SOUL
LASTES FOR THREE MONTH AT A
CLIP. NEVET STAGE: CAPE PARRY

cape Bathurst

FEATURING
AVIATIC LTD
AVIATIC NORTHERNUNION
INTERNATIONAL
WIDE WEAR CORP.
CLOTHING DEPARTMENT
JACKET & TOPS

Globe
GLOBE

Héraldique
HERALDIC

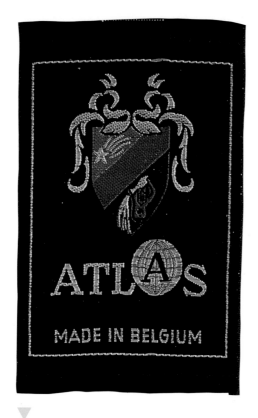

Classiques! Blasons, écussons, armoiries ne sont pas seulement réservés aux BCBG, NAP et autres preppies. Ils servent aussi à des créateurs tels que J.-P. Gaultier qui a relancé le thème médiéval.

The classics! Shields, badges, and the emblems of ancient heraldry aren't just for the N.A.P. and preppies. Designers like J.-P. Gaultier, who has re-introduced the medieval theme, are finding plenty of uses for them.

Héraldique
HERALDIC

▲

◆

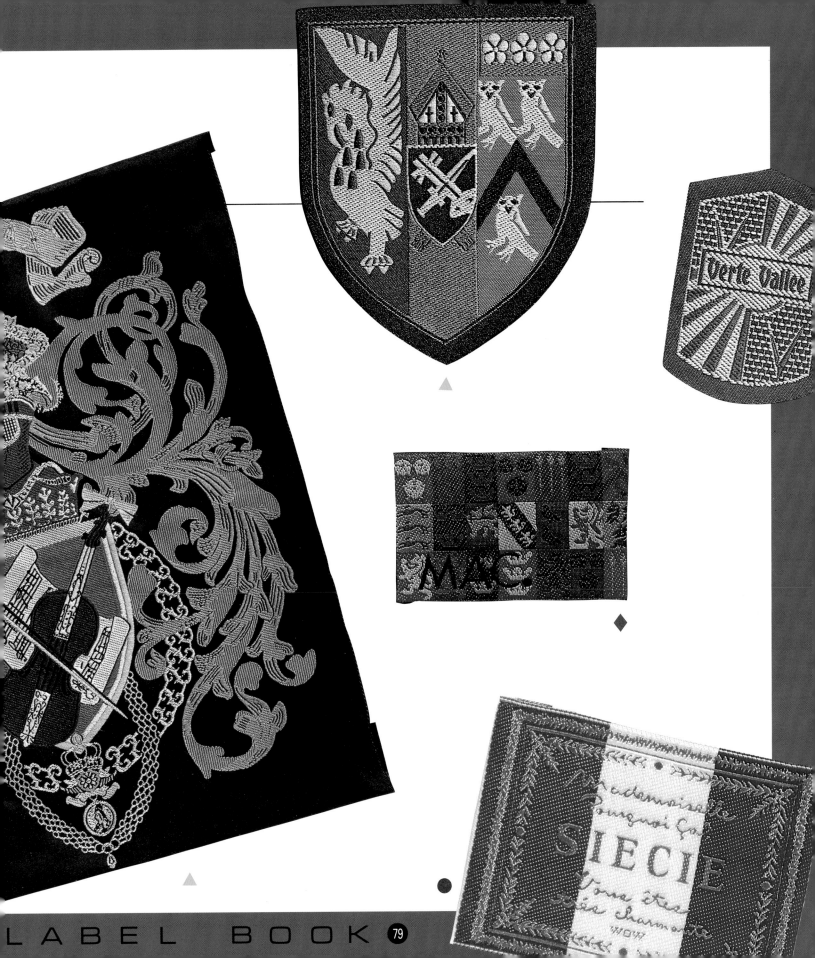

Héraldique
HERALDIC

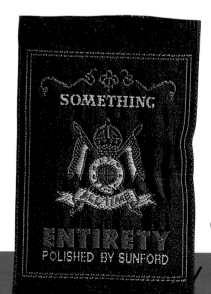

FACTORY ATELIER DE GRANDE MARQUE

NORWAY

Rita Marlow

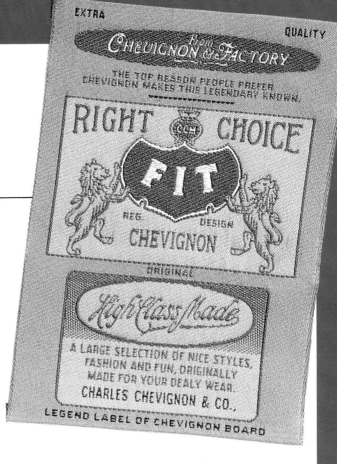

Chevignon from Factory

THE TOP REASON PEOPLE PREFER
CHEVIGNON MAKES THIS LEGENDARY KNOWN.

RIGHT CHOICE

FIT

REG. DESIGN

CHEVIGNON

ORIGINAL

High Class Made

A LARGE SELECTION OF NICE STYLES,
FASHION AND FUN, ORIGINALLY
MADE FOR YOUR DEALY WEAR.

CHARLES CHEVIGNON & CO.,

LEGEND LABEL OF CHEVIGNON BOARD

BESSEG

5

U.S. NAVAL
ACADEMY
ANNAPOLIS, MD.

FOR
MOVING
CHILDREN

tony box

SAC EXP

MODERN
BASIC

S
C

AUTHENTIC
DESIGN

OUR AIM IS TO PRODUCE AN UN
IQUE EQUIPMENT. IDEAS COME FROM EVE
RY CORNER OF THE WORLD. NO. 4780449

Junior

JUNIOR

Aux bébés, les animaux et les poupons naïvement dessinés. Les "juniors", eux, ont droit à des illustrations plus réalistes. On notera la naissance des étiquettes en relief (grâce à l'injection de fils polyamide). Au fait, où est mon Teddy Bear?

For the junior set, realistic designs of animals and babies. Youngsters need something they can understand. Note the new addition: raised labels (using polyamide fiber injection). "Anybody seen my teddy bear?"

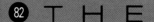

Junior
JUNIOR

© P.I.B./CASTERMAN

BEN TEDDY BEAR
LOVE ME
O12 ®

O12 ben

Ouah!

CHICCO Nurserie

EVEMARIAGE   THE SKY
WITH STAR

IF YOU REALLY LOVE YOUR CHILD, YOU'
TO SEND HIM OUT INTO THE WORLD ON

Locomotion

TRANSPORTS

Un casse-tête, les transports ! On
ne compte pas les dessins qu'ils
ont inspirés. Ici sont uniquement
regroupés ceux qui ont trait aux
moyens de locomotion terrestre.
Un thème sur les chapeaux de
roues.

Transportation is always with us
— it has inspired endless
numbers of designs. Here we give
you only themes connected with
ground transportation. A theme on
wheels.

Locomotion
TRANSPORTS

di mauro

O'NEILL

Locomotion
TRANSPORTS

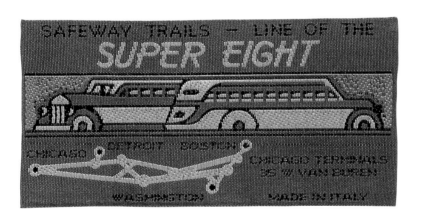

Marine
NAUTICAL

Les marins, les bateaux, la pêche, la vie des transatlantiques... Mais aussi, toute une page consacrée à des rubans du début du siècle destinés aux casquettes des matelots et décorées du nom de leurs navires.

Sailors, ships, fishing boats, transatlantic liners... plus a whole page of early 20th century bands designed for sailor caps and sometimes including the name of the ship.

Jean Leduc

BEST-S PROJECT
PRODUCED BY ISAMU CO.,LTD.

TRANSATLANTIQUE

Giuliano
tricot
MADE IN ITALY

LEVI STRAUSS & Co

Danhartu
BRAND

ROMANTIC WEAR
MANUFACTURED FOR

TOUGH AMERICA FOLKS
COUNTRY
MADE IN ITALY
ORIGINAL JEANS CLOTHING

Marine
NAUTICAL

ROYAL
AUSTRALIAN
NAVY

LEEWARD

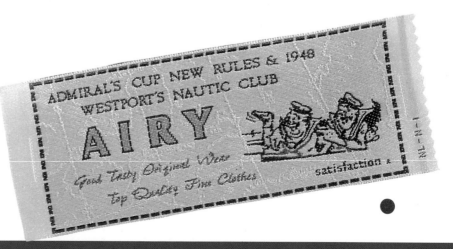

OLD WEAVE BRAND

ROYAL BLUE

PACIFIC TRAIL

TRADE MARK

GARMENT

IMPERIAL

NAVY COAT
GUARANTEED

TO TRAVEL

With Marine's WAG Boat

SAILOR'S

BIG GAME FISHING
REGISTERED TRADE MARK

Marine
NAUTICAL

 Vittorio Emanuele III

Marine
NAUTICAL

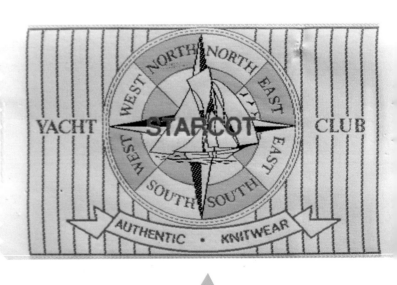

Nature

NATURE

U ne bouffée d'air frais dans ce
thème, on s'évade et on admire
les superbes paysages.
On pourrait presque s'allonger sur
l'herbe, enivré par le parfum des
fleurs…

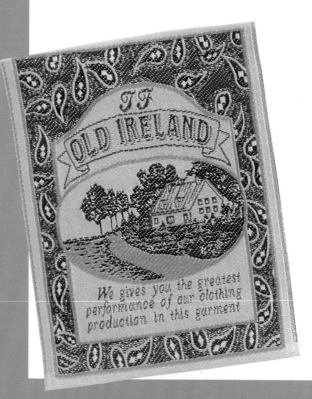

A breath of fresh air for
a get-away-from-it-all,
see-the-world theme. You can
almost feel the grass under your feet
and smell the flowers…

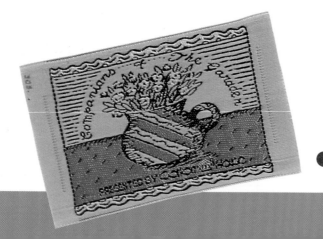

Nature

NATURE

MAKES YOU HAPPY

Nature

NATURE

Casimodo

NAJ-OLEARI
MADE IN ITALY

BETTER FITTING

Simple L

LES TOITS DU MONDE

PÊCHE CHASSE

Fabriqué en France

LA SOC

Sports

SPORTS

COMPOSITION by KENZO TAKADA

U ne des sources d'inspiration les plus constantes qui donne certains des plus beaux chefs-d'œuvre tissés. Nous avons classé les sports par genre, pour donner plus de force à ce thème; à vos marques!... Prêts.

S ports have traditionally served as one of the richest sources of inspiration for woven labels and badges. We've arranged them by category to give more punch to this theme... on your mark, get set... GO!

Sports

SPORTS

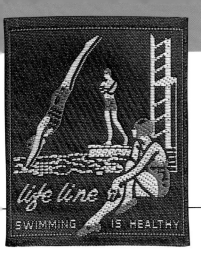

life line
SWIMMING IS HEALTHY

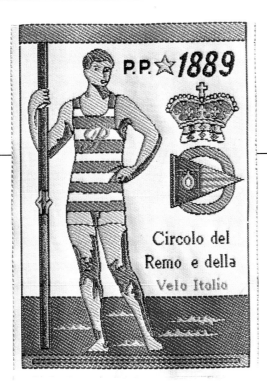

P.P. ☆ 1889

Circolo del
Remo e della
Velo Italio

SINCE 1882
SASSON
NEW YORK
PARIS

ROWING BY SAILOR'S

Lake Casitas
VENTURE COUNTY
OLYMPIC CANOEING

SAC

WORLD CHAMPIONSHIP JAPAN

Henry Cotton's
ORIGINAL OUTDOOR GARMENTS
Rainwear & Sportswear
Clothing
REGISTERED TRADE MARK

Sports
SPORTS

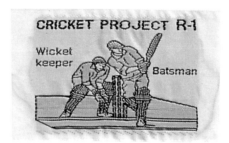

Get the best place
at the horserace !

caramelo

Sports

SPORTS

MADE IN   ITALY

FABBRICATO CON MODERNE TECNICHE NEL RISPETTO
DELLA QUALITÀ E DELLA TRADIZIONE DA

Belfe

SPECIALISTA IN ABBIGLIAMENTO ED ACCESSORI
PER LO SPORT ED IL TEMPO LIBERO

«RAGAZZO KNITTING MILLS»

Retro Spective Collection

CASON CITY FIGHTERS U.S.A.

ONTPELIER SPORTS CLUB

PRODUCED BY CLAUDE CROSS

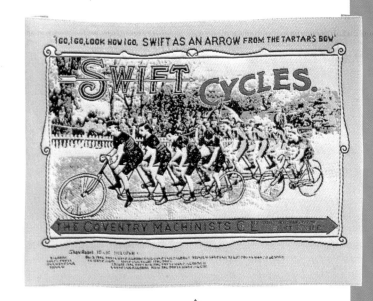

"I GO, I GO, LOOK HOW I GO, SWIFT AS AN ARROW FROM THE TARTARS BOW"

SWIFT CYCLES.

THE COVENTRY MACHINISTS C L.

Typo

TYPO

Elément de choix, ces étiquettes illustrées d'enluminures, de calligraphies, de lettrages déformés, de titres de journaux, sont très en vogue. Comme si saturé d'images, on redécouvrait les vertus de la typographie.

These superb labels are based on old maps and pictures, calligraphy, exaggerated print, newspaper headlines, etc. May be we've had enough of pictures and yearn for print — which would explain the current demand for this type of label.

Typo
TYPO

Jeeper
CARGO AIR TRANSPORT
CIVILIAN SPECIFICATION
PANT MAN'S COTTON
NYLON & LEATHEROC 107
MILJ-701502-
8405-753-6195
SIZE RECULAR-
DRY CLEAN ONLY
DIESEL LTD ®

OUTDOOR WEAR
quality   product
FREEP'S
TRADE   MARK
CLASSIC
CUT
IT'S TAILORED
FOR PERFECT FIT
and Comfort
FOR
OUTDOORSMEN

SELEC
PASS
SUPER HITS DESIG

AUTHENTIC
BASIC DESIGN

LA TENDA ROSSA ®
19 FA 26
TECHNICAL LABEL
AUTHENTIC WARM JACKET
GENUINE MATERIALS   SAFETY PRODUCT
THIS GARMENT IS RECOMMENDED FOR YOUR SAFETY
AND YOUR DURABILITY. TESTED & APPROVED TO SURVIVE
GUARANTEED EVERY TIME

RETRO
VERSO
By Chemin ®
de Campagne
Diffusion
Trade   Mark

TRADITIONAL DE LUXE FABRIC
TRD
PARIS
MADE IN FRANCE

Typo

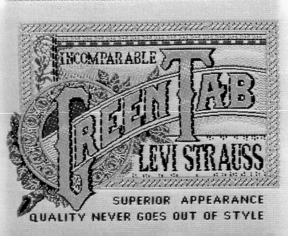

UTILITY
GOLDIE
NOT SO NORMAL

VERTE VALLEE

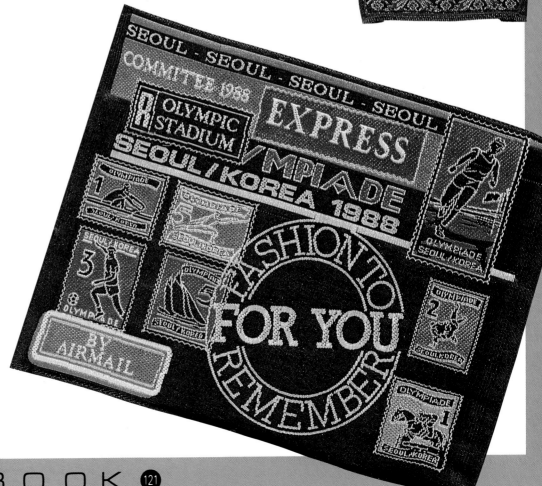

SEOUL - SEOUL - SEOUL - SEOUL
COMMITTEE 1988
OLYMPIC STADIUM
EXPRESS
SEOUL / KOREA 1988
OLYMPIADE
FASHION TO FOR YOU REMEMBER
BY AIRMAIL

Typo
TYPO

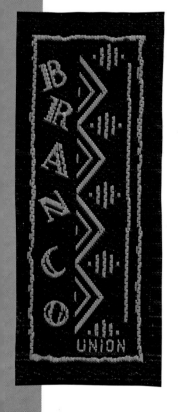

UNION

IN 1860 WE SOLD
100,000 LABELS
IN 1870 WE SOLD
500,000 LABELS
IN 1880 WE SOLD
900,000 LABELS
IN 1895 WE SOLD
2,519,856
LABELS

UNITED
OF BENETTON

VELENO®

STUDIO
0001
BY
FERRE
MADE IN ITALY

CODE
BLEU
JAPAN

100% 100%
COTTON COTON
S
MADE IN JAPAN
FABRIQUE AU JAPON

SPORTING GEAR HAI

SPORTING
GEAR
HAI

CHIPIE

PURE CRISP COTTON

Textile

TEXTILE

E ven the plain old
fabric care or fabric
content label can be
interesting. You don't
believe it? Take a look!

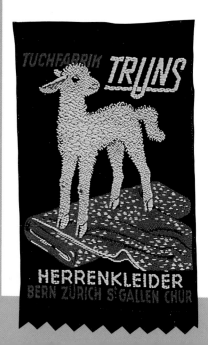

N on, les étiquettes
techniques, les
informations sur la
matière ou les conseils
d'entretien ne sont pas
forcément anodins.
La preuve?
Vous la trouverez ici!

LEVI'S® WASH 'EM HOT INSIDE OUT WASH SEPARATE

WASH AND TUMBLE DRY FOR SOFTER JEANS USE SOFTENER IN RINSE CYCLE

THE MORE YOU WASH 'EM THE BETTER THEY LOOK AND FIT!

TRADITIONAL ® Cashmere NEW WOOL 40% 60% ACCESSORIES DEPARTMENT

MUSTANG WORK

WE A TOUGH & DURABLE GUARANTEE REAL COMFORT

These working clothes are made of good material, handsomely finished and durable tailored.

RAILS
TRANS EXPRESS CLOTHING
LEATHER CLEANING
ONLY BY SPECIALISTS,
WHO ARE COMPETENT
OF TAKING RESPONSIBILITY
——————
NETTOYAGE PAR SPECIALISE

Obey Line
PURE WOOL

Irish Linen

WOVEN IN IRELAND

WE TAKE PURE NEW YARNS AND SEND IT
TO OUR HANDWEAVERS WHO USE THEIR HEREDITARY
SKILL AND WOVEN HANDLOOMS TO PRODUCE THIS
BEAUTIFUL CLOTH EXPRESSLY FOR HENRY COTTON'S

Henry Cotton's NATURAL YARNS

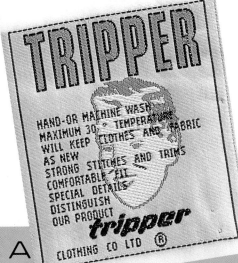

TRIPPER

HAND- OR MACHINE WASH
MAXIMUM 30° TEMPERATURE
WILL KEEP CLOTHES AND FABRIC
AS NEW
STRONG STITCHES AND TRIMS
COMFORTABLE FIT
SPECIAL DETAILS
DISTINGUISH
OUR PRODUCT
tripper
CLOTHING CO LTD ®

Wool and Alpaca

Textile

TEXTILE

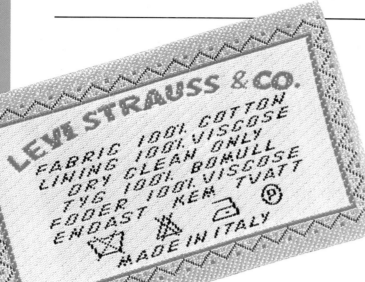

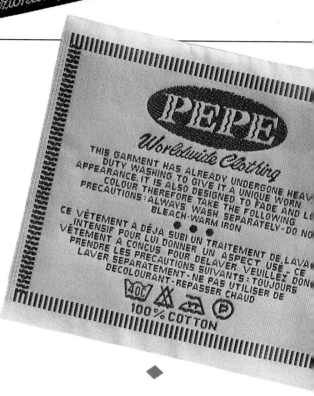

CHARFREY
Genuine leather 1 choice*
Quality of trade

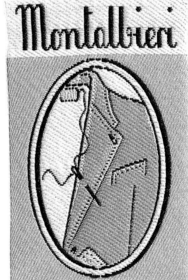

Montalbieri

disegnata da Romano Ridolfi
prodotta da forall

SASCH®

THE PARTICULAR
FINISHING TREATMENT
PERMITS TO WASH THIS
PIECE OF GARMENT QUITE
FREQUENTLY KEEPING IT
PRACTICALLY NEW.

HING CO LTD -
PPER®
STERLY LIFESTYLE
NE - FIT

RFORMANCE

WASH SEPARATELY
TO ORIGINAL

SHING

DENIM BASICS
AS BASICS
SE BLEACH

TDOOR CLOTHES
CO LTD

STERED TRADEMARK

RN00A72/ CAC

Wool and Mohair

Nostalgie
NOSTALGIA

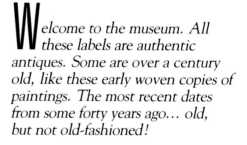

Bienvenue dans notre Musée. Toutes ces étiquettes sont anciennes et authentiques. Elles ont parfois plus d'un siècle, comme ces premiers chefs-d'œuvre tissés d'après tableaux. Ou, au moins une quarantaine d'années. Vieilles, mais pas démodées!…

Welcome to the museum. All these labels are authentic antiques. Some are over a century old, like these early woven copies of paintings. The most recent dates from some forty years ago… old, but not old-fashioned!

La Vogue
SPORT VILLE
16 à 20 Bd ST DENIS
PARIS

MARQUE DÉPOSÉE
GLOBE

IMPERIAL

16 AVENUE DE LA
MESTRE & BLATGÉ
GRANDE ARMÉE

L'Idéal Confort
MARQUE DÉPOSÉE

Compagnie des Indes

Nostalgie
NOSTALGIA

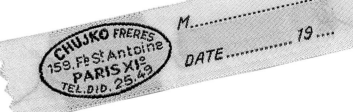

INDÉGORGEABLE

TISSÉ MAIN

TH. OLSSON
HERR-OCH-DAMSKRÄDDERI
STOCKHOLM
___ Namn _____ Dat ___

CORSETS SUR MESURE
Violette Klein
30, Rue Laurent - MULHOUSE

NE PAS REPASSER

INFROISSABLE

INDEMAILLABLE

LA S LORRAINE

AIX
EN-PROVENCE

Cancan
PARIS
MARQUE ET MODELE
DÉPOSÉS

TISSU
Clotex
DÉPOSÉ
G

Kanter's
REG. TRADE MARK

Kanter's
STYLE SIZE

St GERMAIN DES PRÉS

R.C.MEAUX
2.471
REF. N° FACT. N°

INDICATIF GROSSISTE
RAYONNE

Nostalgie
NOSTALGIA

D'APRES E. MUNIER

Nostalgie

Dévidage de la Soie   Pl.2

Neyret Frères et Cⁱᵉ

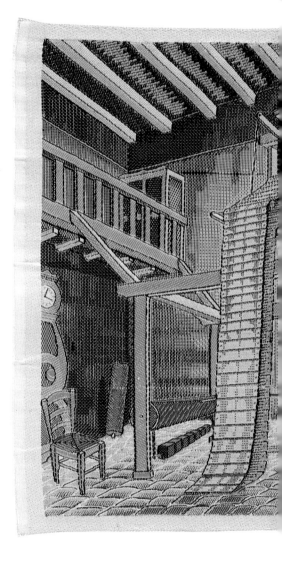

TISSE PAR NEYRET FRERES & Cᵉ   SAINT ETIENNE

Nostalgie
NOSTALGIA

CAMEL HAIRS

ALPALAINE
ALPAGA et LAINE GARANTIS

JUMEL GARANTI
DÉPOSE
IRRETRÉCISSABLE
DEUX FILS

GALERIES LAFAYETTE
PURE LAINE
IRRETRECISSABLE

Selimixte
FAB'on SELITEX

REGISTERED
Comet
TRADE MARK

Paris-Nouveautés
LAVAL
5 et 7, Rue de Rennes

Nostalgie

NOSTALGIA

RUVEN FEDER

Styliste, graphiste et designer, il crée des collections pour quelques-unes des plus grandes marques du prêt-à-porter et du sport.
Depuis le milieu des années 80, son studio de création se spécialise dans le concept de marquage et l'animation du vêtement.
En 87, il a l'idée de créer un nouveau style de cahier de tendances consacré aux logos, badges et étiquettes.
Il prend J.-M. Glasman comme partenaire pour développer ensemble ce projet.
Aujourd'hui, "Logos Designs" est devenu la référence incontournable dans ce domaine.

Stylist, graphic artist, and designer, Ruven Feder has created collections for some of the major names in "prêt-à-porter" and sports apparel.
In the mid-1980's, Ruven Feder and his design studio began their pioneering work in brand name concept and clothing personalization design.
In 1987, he developed a new type of trend book devoted entirely to logos, badges, and labels.
For the successful realization of the new project, he entered into partnership with Jean-Michel Glasman.
Today, "Logos Designs" has become the leading reference work in the field.

J.M. GLASMAN

Véritable chef d'orchestre de la mode, il est partout à la fois.
Styliste, consultant mode et conseil en communication, avec Secret Service Style, la société qu'il dirige.
Il est également à l'origine de Fashion Impact, un des premiers bureaux d'étude d'ordinateurs graphiques appliqués à l'industrie textile.
Enfin, depuis 87, Jean-Michel Glasman édite avec Ruven Feder : "Logos Designs", "le" cahier de tendances de l'étiquette.

Like a conductor with a orchestra to lead, Jean-Michel Glasman is everywhere at once.
He heads Secret Service Style fashion consultants, himself working as stylist and fashion and communications consultant.
He also founded Fashion Impact, one of the first studios providing Computer Assisted Graphics for the textile industry.
And, he has also been working since 1987 in partnership with Ruven Feder on their joint publication "Logos Designs"- The label trend book.

Ce livre vous a plu?
Nous en sommes ravis. Alors, nous vous retrouverons très prochainement dans les pages d'un nouveau volume consacré cette fois à des étiquettes d'un autre genre…

Did you like this book?
We hope so. We'll be seeing you again soon, in the pages of our next book, which will cover other kinds of labels…

WOVEN LABEL BOOK

REMERCIEMENTS
SPECIAL THANKS

Nous remercions tous les fabricants d'étiquettes européens et internationaux qui ont bien voulu nous ouvrir leurs archives,
les marques citées dans la rubrique "à chaque vêtement", qui nous ont confié leurs plus belles étiquettes.
Nous remercions également "le Musée du tissage" à Lyon pour toutes les informations concernant M. Jacquard.

We would like to thank all the label manufacturers from Europe and thoughout the world who opened their archives to us.
Special thanks to the individuals and companies listed in the "To Each Garment Its Own" section, who let us have the finest examples of their products.
We also wish to thank the "Musée du Tissage" of Lyon for all information concerning Monsieur Jacquard.